I0410682

A HANDBOOK OF HISTORIC CEMETERY RECOVERY

A HANDBOOK OF HISTORIC CEMETERY RECOVERY

By: John G. Edmonds

The author, in uniform, talking to John Ward left and Bill Keys outside the door to courtroom "A" in the Old Courthouse in Redwood City. Ward was a member of the Board of Supervisors and Keys was the Police Chief for the City of Hillsborough. I don't remember why we were together at that time

It was a surprise visit.

As I was sitting in my bailiff chair during a trial in courtroom "A" in the old courthouse in San Mateo County, a frail redheaded woman walked up to me and whispered if I could come outside for a minute. The trial was a civil case and rather boring so I readily agreed to join her.

We went into the rotunda where three courtrooms are situated. This 85 year old woman stood as if she were 25. The sun shone through the flag windows in the rotunda and sparkled off her red hair, her blue eyes sparkling like the sun. She had a purpose and a determination that was almost irresistible and I thought to myself that I had little choice in the matter at hand.

Her name was Jean Cloud and what I did not know at the time was that her visit would change my life. When I was a child of 7 or 8 this woman came to Washington School, an elementary school on Woodside Road, in Redwood City. My class suddenly found itself in the auditorium learning to folk dance. While I did not remember her at the time she remembered me but that probably wasn't because of the dance class. It was more likely because of many years of publicity related to my law enforcement efforts as a Deputy Sheriff.

Mrs. Jean Cloud, a dear friend and helper, died at 103 and committed me to completing the work in the cemetery.

I had written a small booklet, at the request of the court administrator, on the history of the courts in Redwood City. The purpose was to celebrate the resurrection of the beautiful glass dome that had been in disrepair because of earthquake activity. Included in the booklet were two of the judges, who sat in judgment since the first such building was established in 1858 on that property. Jean Cloud explained that Union Cemetery on Woodside Road was badly in need of some tender loving care. I had grown up near that cemetery and had been in it many times. She told me that during the last 20 years the cemetery had been badly vandalized. I had driven by many times in my patrol car and was very much aware of the increasing destruction of the monuments. Jean stated she wanted to start an organization that would rehabilitate and repair the stones. Jean reminded me that both Judge Benjamin Fox, the county's first judge and Judge George Buck, the county's longest tenured judge, are buried in Union Cemetery, judges I had written about in the original booklet.

I agreed to help, not knowing that it would become an absolute addiction. Sometimes addictions of this sort are not a bad thing although this certainly took me away from my family more often than I should have allowed. Jean Cloud was a very nice elderly lady with a wide smile and the kind of attitude that makes saying "no" to her very difficult. We were standing in that beautiful old courthouse with its colorful stained glass dome and stained glass windows high above the floor. It was a majestic scene that would repeat itself in my mind for the rest of my life.

I met with two other people, Helen Graves and Francis Hutchinson and we discussed what we would need to do to repair the cemetery. In many cases, the gravestones were broken into pieces or had disappeared. I volunteered that we needed a substantially larger organization to begin with and suggested that we go to all the historical organizations in the city and see if we could find four or five more people who would be interested in joining such an organization. We found quite a few people who were in-

This was the first Eagle Scout program we did and Lars Lysand did a wonderful job on the fence.

terested and about eight more people who would be part of a board of directors. We met and established the "Historic Union Cemetery Association."

The Cooley-Frisbie plot was the first Eagle Scout project. The fences were mostly flat on the ground.

The year was 1994 and Union Cemetery had already been placed on the National Register of Historic Places, this having occurred in 1967, even though it was in such a rough condition. The cemetery had been organized in 1859 because of an urgent need. Burials had taken place on the property of Horace Hawes, a state legislator, who traveled often. The property was leased and the resident allowed the burials. When Hawes returned he did not approve and told the community that the bodies would have to be exhumed. Hawes agreed to contribute to the cause if a suitable burial ground could be located.

A committee was established made up of Charles Fox, Jerome Turner and Charles Ayers. All are permanent residents of Union Cemetery. The committee was able to purchase, following government approval and funding, a six acre parcel on Woodside Road just west of El Camino Real. The property was purchased from Curtis Baird and Alan Berry who bought it from Simon Mezes who had been the Mexican grant owner, having earned it from the Arguello family, as their attorney.

The property was purchased for $500 by the Union Cemetery Association. Because there were no certified cities in San Mateo County it was necessary to give the property to the State of California for recording and safe keeping. The exhumations and reburials began immediately. The first was little Annie Douglass who died at age four. There were a total of 13 burials on the original property and over a period of two weeks, the burials were all transferred to Union Cemetery.

Looking toward the Grand Army of the Republic plot from the back side of the Masonic plot in 1970.

The reburials took place in 1859, two years before the start of the Civil War. The cemetery got its name because many men had moved to this area from New England and other eastern states and they were trying to make a statement to the southern sympathizers who were acting out in the vicinity.

Committees were formed three or four times for the purpose of rehabilitating Union Cemetery but little were accomplished. There were a number of reasons for this failure but the least of which was the perpetual disagreement between Nita Spangler and Jean Cloud about how things should be done. Nita wanted survey after survey and she got her wish but

Looking back toward the Grand Army of the Republic's plot from the back side of the Masonic plot. This is the appearance today.

all this surveying did little in terms of actual physical change in the cemetery.

In the spring of 1995 Jean Cloud, Francis (Hutch) Hutchinson, Helen Graves and I sat down with the city manager to talk about the cemetery. The cemetery had been returned to the city by the state in 1964. The city did about as much as the state did in the area of taking care of this burial ground. The four of us informed the city manager that we were going to start working to make improvements and that the city could join us but if they chose not to we would do it ourselves. The cemetery was now designated as a city park and the city had a responsibility. A representative of the Park and Recreation

Committee of the city was assigned to attend our meetings, Ramon Aguilar. Ramon became personally involved and was very helpful.

The Historic Union Cemetery Association started accepting memberships at $10 a year. (This is still the price of membership,) board members were surprised at the number of relatives of people buried in the cemetery who enthusiastically sent in their membership money, many of them sent in substantially more support money as donations. After about a year we had made enough money to make some changes, so we called "Fontana and Company" in Colma, a small city about 20 miles north of us, we asked them to come down and repair six monuments in which we had all the pieces. Workers came down and very generously fixed 16.

The cemetery association sent in the forms and became an official non-profit 501C organization under California State Law. We were able to give Fontana a write off for their work on the additional monuments. We thought this worked out well so a few months later we inquired about repeating this process and Fontana willingly joined us with the committee paying about half and giving Fontana our number for the additional half. This happened a third time a few months later, and the cemetery was starting to look much better. We will forever be in dept to Fontana and Company for its efforts, which continue to date.

This is the Grand Army of the Republic plot at the front of the cemetery. Note: there is

The Grand Army of the Republic Organization, which was started in the East just after the Civil War, developed in Redwood City and was chartered in 1886. They developed a need for a plot in the cemetery and so did the Masonic Chapter. Such plots were established and lawns were planted.

When we started improving the cemetery in 1994, the lawns no longer existed and both areas were just weeds. Also, the original paths that defined the burial plots were gone and plants were growing across largely obliterated paths.

Today the soldier is back, thanks to a Mrs. Williamson who is related to John Poole, a Civil War veteran.

The Grand Army of the Republic had placed its statue of a soldier on a pedestal on the plot. The statue was donated by Mrs. Leland Stanford. Unfortunately, when we started working on the cemetery, the statue had been pulled down and smashed. There were fences around some of the plots but most of the fences had been broken and had parts missing.

We solved these problems by developing a new program for the cemetery; we would help boys who needed a project to win their Eagle awards in the Boy Scouts. Word got around and we soon had some very valuable and capable assistance. The City also joined in the program and put up a substantial wire fence with a gate and a very strong lock. It took a truck to pull the statue down and vehicles cannot enter the cemetery without a key anymore.

A San Mateo Times article reported, "As soldiers go, the one at Union Cemetery wasn't very tough." 'Sure, he guarded over the Grand Army of the Republic soldiers lying in the cemetery's eastern point. He also had his rifle stolen and let vandals get the jump on him three times. Still, folks here hold a soft spot for the nearly 7-foot Civil War soldier and they're hoping to resurrect him this year. The Historic Union Cemetery Association has raised $25,000 to have a sculptor recreate the original.

This stone of the Bottger family illustrates the funery art in Union Cemetery

Union Cemetery, located on Woodside Road (State highway #84) is the final resting place for some 2,400 County pioneers and their descendents. The six acre cemetery dates back to 1859 and is the only cemetery in the County on the National Register and the State list of Historic Landmarks and it boasts considerable amounts of the best examples of Victorian funerary art in the area."

When a scout approaches the committee for a project he is told to meet us at the cemetery and we discuss the options. The boys are then required to decide what needs to be done, and to present the project to the cemetery board. Then it must be presented to the City Park and Recreation Board and then to the Boy Scout officials.

The cemetery association was doing well with donations and lots of people sent in checks in greater amounts than the ten dollars. When people see progress and they feel secure that the money will be well spent, they are willing to make more substantial donations. For example, a Mrs. Williamson donated $20,000 to the association in memory of the Poole Family of which she was a member. This money was used to have the soldier on the Grand Army plot remade and done so in a way that it would never be pulled down again.

It was a great day when the foundry that made the identical new soldier arrived at the cemetery and installed the statue on its pedestal. Francis Hutchinson was dying of inoperable cancer but was able to come to the cemetery to see this ceremony. He was not able to leave the car but he felt, and he said so, that "this was one of the greatest accomplishments of his life." We all agreed. Hutch passed away the next week. His visit to the ceremony was his last.

The Grand Army of the Republic's plot with the $20,000 donation from Mrs. Williamson we were able to reproduce the original and install him in a way that he will never be pulled down again.

But let's stop here and talk a little about the history of this old cemetery. The name, "Union Cemetery" was established in 1859, two years before the start of the American Civil War. The stated reason for this name was the strong feelings of the people who started the cemetery in reference to the continuing threat of secession in the area.

In 1886 the local Grand Army of the Republic chapter was established in Redwood City. This organization was made up entirely of veterans of the Union Army that fought during the Civil War. These returning veterans were aging rapidly and the need for a burial ground was obvious. A site named Union Cemetery was ideal so a special plot was designated a Civil War plot and the veterans were placed there. This resulted in an annual parade and honor day, eventually known as Memorial Day. The walk from the City out to the cemetery with bands and local people involved in the event and observing the always impressive ceremony, this tradition continues today although because of road construction we no longer walk, the event begins at the front gate.

During the 1950s, 60s, 70, and 80s the cemetery was desecrated by vandals who destroyed, without the monuments in the cemetery but they did not destroy the monuments in the Grand Army's plot, although they did destroy the beautiful statue of a union army soldier which adorned the pedestal in the center of the plot.

On May 30, 1966, the Redwood City Tribune printed an article written by Marian Goodman, a staff writer. "Dismal Future for Union Cemetery "Read the headline. "In Redwood City's old Union Cemetery on Woodside Road near Five Points, 45 headstones fringe a little plot centered with a granite-based Civil War figure in bronze. Previously maintained in a red-brown color, last week the veteran figure was covered with gilt paint."

"On the night of Friday May 12, 1957 this priceless monument, even then nearly 100 years old, was pulled down and mutilated by ghoulish vandals.

Our 2nd county judge did not have a tombstone, it was probably wooden and it has disappeared, so Fontana & Co. made him a new stone identical to the original.

Redwood City Police figured it had required an automobile and tow rope to complete this vicious act.

"Though the city and fraternal organizations offered rewards for information leading to the arrest of the vandals, the awards never had to be paid, for the perpetrators were never apprehended."

When the cemetery was established, owner-ship was given to the State of California because there were no certified cities in San Mateo County at the time. The state never took care of the cemetery and just let it deteriorate. In the 1960s Redwood City received the cemetery ownership from the state through a quick claim deed. City officials took up the state's role and did very little to stop the destruction. Several people tried to step in and help but nothing was being accomplished except that they were able to get the cemetery on the National Register of Historic Places in 1983 after five years of lobbying. A number of years later, they also were able to get the cemetery, California State Landmark status.

Sometime in the 1980s a local businessman decided to make some come changes, he applied to the city to tear down the cemetery and make it a Little League Baseball field. It was Jean Cloud and Nita Spangler who addressed the city council and success-fully blocked the process even though the businessman had already brought in a bull dozer and had knocked down a few of the monuments.

The rose is called "Mutablis" and it is an old garden rose that I planted 12 years ago. It's roots found an underground creek and it is now 40 feet around and 12 feet high and still growing.

Several surveys were completed, one by the Native Daughters and another by the University of California. These surveys and a couple of brief history projects resulted in a rather secret understanding of the historic value of the cemetery. However the vandalism continued, pretty much unabated. It wasn't slowed down until the Historic Union Cemetery Association was established in the 1990s and work on rehabilitation was being accomplished that the vandalism started to disappear.

The people we drafted into helping us rehabilitate the cemetery and the things we did to accomplish that goal include:

- Fontana and Company, whose owners and employees literally fell in love with the cemetery, keeps giving us very good prices on tombstones. We try to duplicate the original if possible and place the current year on the bottom right corner of every new stone. This relates to the national register status. The only way we can exactly duplicate the original is if we have a picture and that rarely happens, but we have to try. Unfortunately some of them were probably wooden and have literally disappeared in the 150 years since the cemetery opened.

- The Boy Scouts of America local chapter inquired about Eagle Scout projects in the cemetery. We worked out many ideas and through this process plot fences were restored, lawns in the Grand Army and Masonic plots and paths and roads were restored, many roses were planted, especially along the fence, and ivy was, to some extent, removed. These efforts continue.

- The Audubon Society contacted me about putting bird houses in the oak trees in the cemetery to study the rare California Blue Bird. We agreed and this process continues.

- I joined the Peninsula Rose Society and studied the process of pruning and caring for roses. Lauren Kehoe a San Mateo County judge, asked me to come to her house and remove to the cemetery some 25 roses. She was moving to Florida. I did this and established an area known now as the rose garden in the middle of the cemetery. I also learned how to do cuttings of the old garden roses and grew many of them at home and transplanted them to the cemetery. This process continues. The Rose Society comes to the cemetery every February and prunes the hybrid "T" roses in the rose garden and along the fence paralleling Woodside Road.

- Davies Tree Service, inquired about pruning some of the oak, redwood, pine and pepper trees. They wanted to use the cemetery to train new employees. We arranged to have some trees cut down and most of the trees pruned so that the view into the cemetery from Woodside Road is now much clearer.

This helps to reduce the occasional acts of vandalism that still occur, especially around Halloween.

- Needless to say the cemetery is looking much better. What also helped are the tours we offer school groups. They come for tours but we do not do rubbings however we do photo programs for the kids. We also do quarterly tours for the general public.

- Redwood City Parks and Recreation Department put in drip watering systems for the Hybrid roses and the 44 roses that line the fence along Woodside Road. This reduces the watering requirements because we just need to water the Old Garden roses that are new. The cemetery originally was filled with roses that were planted more than a hundred years ago and without a drip system. I pretty much leave them alone because they bloom beautifully every April and May and require no attention. The drip watering system along the Woodside Road fence was put in by an Eagle Scout and he did a great job.

- Ellen Crawford, a good friend, came to me one fine day and stated that Union Cemetery needed a web-site. She offered to establish one for the cemetery and proceeded to do just that: www.historicunioncemetery.com the site has been a boon to the cemetery association because we have received a substantial number of phone calls from people who have discovered long lost relatives through this site.

The George Solari Windmill

- The Solari Windmill was added to the cemetery in the only area where there were no graves. The city was looking for a place to put the windmill because it was taking up too much space in the corporation yard. The Native Sons of the Golden West decided to rebuild the windmill in this secure location. The windmill is capable of drawing water from Redwood Creek but it is not equipped to do so. All we use it for is to store hoses and other equipment. It comes in very handy for such purposes. Also, it is now located in the closest place possible to its original location.

George Solari was a member of the Native Sons of the Golden West and he owned a farm about a quarter of a mile east of the windmill's present location. Two women worked to get the windmill moved into Union Cemetery. It replaces a watchman's cabin which was lost over the years. There are two plaques on rocks at the entrance to the windmill commemorating the two women but a separate plaque stating the Native Sons role is substantially more accurate.

Eventually, the public interest grew to the extent that Redwood City began working in the cemetery. They now mow the lawns in the Grand Army plot and the Masonic plot. They also put up street lights throughout the cemetery and the original hedge that ran along the highway was removed some time ago and a solid cyclone fence and a gate with a good padlock replaced it. The statue on the Grand Army plot was pulled down and smashed by using a vehicle and a rope. This can't happen anymore because of the fencing and gate.

This is the author of this essay talking to Alicia Aguirre, a member of the city council, before the Memorial Day Ceremony in 2012

I wrote a book on the cemetery, with pages on people buried there   and the towns they came from in the East and where they lived in San Mateo County and their life stories to the extent possible.   The book sold for $20 and we went through five printings in the original form and then it was formally published and we increased the size and the number of people and made it more beautiful. Star Publishers in Redwood City did a wonderful job on putting this improved book out. We sell this book for $20 and it is in its second printing. It is available to the world on Amazon.com.

Memorial Day historically has been a day of celebration at the cemetery. The Grand Army of the Republic met at the Congregational Church and was joined by the Native Sons of the Golden West and Native Daughters of the Golden West as well as high school boys and Girl Scouts carrying the American Flag and many other citizens in a march to the cemetery. Normally the commanding officer of the Grand Army gave a stirring speech and children spread flowers at the grave stones of those who had fallen earlier.

We are joined, on Memorial Day, by the gentlemen of the Order of E. Clampsus Vitas, who enter the cemetery with their Slippery Gulch marching band. It is a colorful occasion with the roses all in bloom, the lawns mowed, the Clampers in   their red and black with pinned vests and the Native Daughters with their ice cream and their flowers for the children to place on the graves. The speakers now are city council members or mayors for the most part. State legislators often ask to speak and we are honored to accept. We sometimes go out and find Civil War speakers who generally don't talk as long as the politicians. Hundreds of people now attend these ceremonies and they enjoy the programs.

Cemetery tours are given several times a year and often more people join us than we have docents available. It is necessary to train more people to give tours. Doing this is certainly my pleasure because as they become more interested, even more people start to involve themselves.

I cannot emphasize enough the importance of involving various other groups in the process of rehabilitation, the more people who become involved the more that will be accomplished. When the cemetery becomes more beautiful it will attract the right kind of people and the amount of vandalism will be reduced.

The cemetery has been so greatly improved that Redwood City decided to hold a Halloween party there recently. The committee working on the project called it a "Haunting" and it was held a week before the Halloween main event in the community. Ten people donated $1,000 each and tickets were $30 each, some 130 people joined us at that price and it turned out to be a huge fund raiser for the cemetery association. It is an honor to assume that our efforts have been rewarded by people just wanting to be in the park. Ghost stories are not hard to come by in those conditions and the party was a great success.

Today we have three Eagle Scout programs in progress. One boy is pulling out plants that have grown beyond their value and another is working on repairing a small plot border fence and a third boy is working to rid the cemetery of the invasive ivy plant.

Another project just established, this week, is a special program for disabled adults. Volunteers will be coming into the cemetery twice a week to pick up litter and do minor cleanup efforts. The city has offered to provide tools and bags for the folks and the city will pick up the litter and take it to its corporation yard for disposal. I am very excited about this program because it makes disabled people feel useful and it helps to keep this park clean.

The disabled also have volunteered to paint the three wooden fences in the cemetery. This is a substantial help because the fences are in need of paint and the city, whose true responsibility it is, just does not have the people available to do this. The cemetery board has agreed to do some preliminary work and the city has agreed to provide the paint and other materials that might be needed.

One of the best ways to help restore historic cemeteries is to solicit descendants if you can find them. It is also valuable to see if there are any old world stone masons who might be able to replicate the original stones. This costs money but often grants are available.

Make the cemetery a city or county park and have the responsible agency invest in it. Through city workers, if you are successful, you can find   experts on flowers in the area, on repairing old roads in the cemetery, on   rehabilitating stones sometimes and on planting and pruning roses, if that is what you wish. People continue to die everywhere and that means there must be businesses in your area that makes tombstones. Solicit their help in the restoration of stones in an historic cemetery.

You make the old cemetery beautiful, by adding colorful plants in the spring and fall and a well organized road or pathway   with places to sit down. Visitors enjoy coming to places that are peaceful and colorful, smell good and just walk or sit down and read, meditate or pray. Descendents especially like to visit relatives and feel so very much better when they recognize their relatives are in a place that the city, county or general public recognize as a real gem of a park in their community.

The second section of this report will include two institutions that I used to write the material for the cemetery book....Union Cemetery, Redwood City California, The People, Their Lives, Their Communities.

The first institution is the Local History Room of the Redwood City Public Library and the Schellens collection, the century old newspapers in which obituaries can often be found. I am aware that many people reading this material may not have opportunities such as the Schellens collection available to them but they may have something similar.

1.   January 21, 1859, William Godfrey sold his San Francisco newspaper, the Mariposa Gazette. The following several months he used to obtain new and improved equipment and he moved down the peninsula to Redwood City and started a new newspaper, The San Mateo County Gazette.

The Redwood City Tribune published an article about the Gazette on April 9, 1959, "San Mateo County Gazette, Vol.1, No.1, Saturday Morning April 9, 1857. An independent weekly journal devoted to news, literature, agriculture and the local interests of San Mateo County. The paper will be published every Saturday morning by David Downer, editor and proprietor. Office, in the Odd Fellows Hall corner of "A" and Third streets, this

city. Subscriptions: $4 a year in advance. L. P. Fisher, 620 Washington Street, William B. Lake, corner Washington and Montgomery Streets, San Francisco are authorized to receive advertisements for this paper and collect payments therefore."

Herman Ambrose Scofield was born in Vermont on the first day of September, 1819. He was educated in his native state and came to California with his attorney shingle and an interest in looking for gold. He engaged in mining in Placer and Nevada Counties and was successful but the backbreaking work caused him to haul his riches to San Mateo County and

to settle in Redwood City. He had been
elected Justice of the Peace in Auburn and he
was qualified to practice law anywhere in California.

Herman Scofield was elected District Attorney of San Mateo County in 1863 and
served for two years, one full term. Following
his political efforts Herman became the owner
of the San Mateo County Gazette. One of his
first reports in the paper was that of his own
sorrow, "The San Mateo County Gazette reported on 12-24-1867 the death of Mrs. Lucy
Ann Fargo Scofield, wife of Herman A. Scofield,
editor of this paper, at the age of 43. Native of
Rutland, Vermont.

In November of 1871 Scofield moved the
newspaper business out of its first building
then into a new building which became known
as the "Time-Gazette Building" still on the east
side of Main Street.

Scofield continued running the newspaper even after he was elected Justice of the
Peace for the third township. He stayed with
these jobs until his death at age 61 on January

13, 1881. He was buried in plot 53 in Union Cemetery.

On September 9, 1885, Ralph Sidney Smith, who served his apprenticeship with the Times Gazette, became the editor of the paper and continued to write for the paper after Dennis O'Keefe bought the paper.

Times-Gazette building on Main Street in Redwood City.

We had the pleasure of presenting our favorite man to the Board of Supervisors the other day. He is Dennis E. O'Keefe of Menlo Park. We introduced him as dean of the county press and unless someone can claim county newspaper service before 1893, the title is unchallenged ... Dennis and James O'Keefe acquired the newspaper in 1893 (San

Mateo County Times-Gazette). In 1906 Dennis O'Keefe became sole owner. He was active editor and publisher and leased the paper to the Redwood City Tribune. Each week he used to send in a list of personnel items from Menlo Park in the penciled longhand of the pioneer editor and just as bright and chipper too. It used to be one of my chores to type them so that modern day typesetters could have what they call "clean copy." Finally they stopped. A couple of years ago he sold the property to the Tribune outright, retaining possession of the bound volumes from 1859 to 1931. He appeared before the board to give these volumes to the county library on behalf of the people of San Mateo County. Since there is no other source book for a concise history of the county during this period. The gift is invaluable particularly if you are interested in the history of this period. One of the volumes is missing 1904-5 and some of the others have been mutilated. In return for Mr. O'Keefe's generosity the county has voted enough money to prepare a bronze plaque which will perpetuate the memory of the donor of the O'Keefe collection of the Times-Gazette.

J. V. Swift, newspaper editor

The O'Keefe family came to San Francisco from their native, Ireland   Dennis and James, identical twins, were born in a house on Jessie Street in San Francisco but the family moved and settled on Oak Grove Avenue in Menlo Park. The brothers were educated in the local schools while their father farmed where Stanford University now stands. Dennis did everything on the Times Gazette, editing, writing, bookkeeping managing and anything else that came into focus. Among his supporters and subscribers were Leland Stanford, Senator Latham, James L. Flood, Senator Gelton, Alvinza Hayward, Herbert Hoover and Denis Martin of Searsville. Denis Martin was a good friend of Dennis O'Keefe and later remembered attending a church serves at St. Denis out at Searsville.

Redwood City Tribune, August 2, 1950: "Dennis E. O'Keefe was honored at a plaque unveiling here. He was honored at a ceremony in the County Redwood City Library yesterday afternoon. About 50 people attended the unveiling of a plaque designating the bound volumes of the Times-Gazette, the County's first newspaper, there were county officials, librarians and many of Redwood City's elder citizens were present. The occasion was the unveiling of a plaque designating the bound volumes of the Times-Gazette the county's first newspaper to be named the O'Keefe Collection. The first issue of the Redwood City Tribune was 1931-1932."

The bound newspapers that Dennis O'Keefe donated, The O'Keefe Collection, have been extremely valuable for doing stories from the Civil War, the Lincoln Assassination and about anything else that was newsworthy from that period up to 1932.

James Vincent Smith started as an apprentice with the Times – Gazette and gradually grew in stature. When the times – Gazette was sold Swift bought into the Redwood City Democrat and he became full owner and editor on January 7, 1904. The newspapers offices and building backed onto Redwood Creek. It was a pretty location with yearlong flowing water and pleasant sounds to make the hard work of printing a newspaper a good deal more pleasant. In February 1913, Swift became something of a hero when he heard the despairing cackle of a hen, drowning in the creek. Swift dove into the swollen torrent to rescue the distressed bird. Then, with rare presence of mind, he dispatched the office-boy to a saloon for a flask of brandy with which to resuscitate the fowl. Swift had been composing an editorial when the hen's predicament stirred him to action. Redwood Creek was swollen from the recent rain and had caught the distressed fowl in an overflow and was carrying it away, clucking in indignant protest past the office of the Democrat on Broadway.

"No chicken ever appealed to me in vain," wrote Swift later. "The editor's heroic act was witnessed by an admiring throng, and public sentiment in Redwood City is all for immortalizing the deed in some substantial manner." -- The San Francisco Examiner Tuesday February 25, 1913.

Swift was born in the city of West Union to Miles and Rose Swift who immigrated to West Union from their native Ireland.

It must be noted that the volumes of 150 year old newspapers are getting increasingly fragile and in some cases are torn; indeed in several cases people have cut articles out of the paper. These papers are precious and they will be even more valuable to future generations if we take good care of them today. James Vincent Smith also did his public duties by spending four terms as a Redwood City councilman and one term as its mayor. He also was on the elementary school board. James is buried in Holy Cross Cemetery in Menlo Park, California.

The Redwood City Democrat noted on April, 29, 1915 that J. V. Swift was retiring from the newspaper. "The Democrat took a new associate editor, James D. Hedge, the general management of the paper resting with him. Along with the announcement came this remark from Mr. J. V. Swift, 'With this issue of the Democrat, its owner, who for the past sixteen years had guided its destinies, retires to take up the less active and perhaps less pleasant occupation of managing the local post office. While surrendering active management the owner will continue to mold its policies.'"

The Shellens Collection, Local history and individual history on the left and other counties in California on the right. The San Francisco collection, which is extensive, is in the vault.

2.   The second institution to be discussed is the Redwood City Public Library and Local History Room. I start by stating that the Redwood City Public Library just received a 5 star rating by the people who do those sorts of things and only two libraries, apparently, in the United States received that top rating. It is a library worth visiting. The local history room is also a good place to visit but its hours are limited because it is being run, during these times of recession, by volunteers. It is open between 1PM and 4PM Monday through Thursday.

Richard N. Schellens

The local history room contains bound newspapers dating back to 1859; the O'Keefe Collection is invaluable for local and even some national history. The papers are invaluable for finding obituaries for people buried in Union Cemetery.

Richard N. Schellens, the "History Detective." I am hard pressed to call the people on the television program of the same name as this, as true history detectives. A large retinue of people who do the research and put together the program (which I enjoy very much) are the real backbone of the program. The "stars" merely follow the steps of the researchers, as they go from one end of the country to the other.

Redwood City had a real history detective. The Redwood City Tribune published an article in 1964 titled, "Schellens, Ace Historical Detective."

I am speaking of Richard N. Schellens, who was the author of an astounding amount of historical information about Redwood City, the Peninsula, San Francisco, the State of California and almost every county in this state. It takes up an immense amount of space in the Local History Room in the Redwood City Public Library, on the mezzanine level.

The binding that Dennis O'Keefe put on the edition
from 1859 to 1931 of the Times Gazette
newspapers....they were Saturday issues once
weekly during that period and they are very fragile.

I've been using the work of Richard Schellens for a number of years, especially when working on books such as the book on Union Cemetery. While the collection is not perfect, it is close to that. However, I do find people in the cemetery who just did not seem to have great public lives. Schellens seems to disregard some people, or else he simply did not find the information to give to us. Following his retirement from a cement plant job, he spent a substantial amount of time in the Redwood City Tribune's research rooms looking for people, places and things in old newspapers. He often contributed material for columns in the Tribune. Otto Tallent, a well known editor of the Tribune, talked about Henry D. McGarvey, who donated property for the American Legion Hall on El Camino in the north part of Redwood City. Schellens talked to him about Henry, but he went on to tell him about Owen McGarvey, Henry's father, who moved to this area in the 1850s. Owen purchased 1,000 acres from the Arguellos, the original Mexican grant owners, and established his home in the property now known as the Menlo Country Club. Owen McGarvey rests in Union Cemetery.

He also told the paper about the quick silver mine Owen found in the Searsville area and how he then used the gravel of the mine to cover the roads in Redwood City to reduce the winter mud and the summer dust.

Richard Schellens was born in Los Angeles and was two-and-a-half years old when he was adopted by Mr. and Mrs. Richard Schellens. Mrs. Anna Schellens purchased land in what we call Emerald Lake area of Redwood City and the family moved north.

Richard Schellens' speech had a noticeable German accent to it in his later days. His parents spoke German and his father was a native of Cologne and an engineer of railroad systems. He became quite wealthy having built a rail system for the emperor of China.

The Schellens family sold their property in Redwood City and travelled back to Germany in 1920 where they placed young Richard in grammar school. They then returned to California in 1924, settling first in Palo Alto.

Richard Schellens had been unaware for most of his life that he had been adopted. When he went down to Los Angeles he looked up his records and he discovered his birthplace and hospital and he found that two babies had been born on his birthday. One had light and the other, dark hair. He learned then that his real name had been William Robert Brooks. The only parents he ever really knew were the Schellens, so he kept the name.

The Schellens family traveled constantly, living on the dividends from the father's stock investments. In 1929, Richard enrolled in a junior college in Asheville, North Carolina and upon completion; he came back to California and enrolled in the University of California at Los Angeles for two years. Then he returned to Germany and went back to school for two more years at the University of Munich, where he studied economics and observed the rise of Adolph Hitler.

Richard returned to California and got a job working for McNeil and Libby in Sunnyvale and Sacramento. In 1940 he went back to school, working his way through Stanford University to earn a credential to teach, his work was selling copper stock for the Kennecott Copper Company. His education was interrupted, by the beginning of the Second World War. Richard found himself in the finance section of the United States Army. He was stationed in Honolulu. His job was to escort the military payroll when it was flown to the South Pacific basis.

A photo of the binders that are contained in the boxes on the shelves in the picture above. They contain a plethora of information of historic value about people in Redwood City and far beyond. It is a collection that any historian interested in western history should wish to visit the Local History Room.

After the war and a period of recuperation from an illness, Richard went to work for the Portland Cement Company, which later became the Ideal Cement Company, in Redwood City. He worked for 14 years and retired in 1960 and began, "to look for something worthwhile to keep my brain occupied." That is when he launched his research of the South Peninsula and Redwood City and then expanded in a grand way by doing the newspaper histories of all California counties.

These are the photo drawers in which a researcher can find thousands of photographs on all sorts of subjects. But you better bring your scanner.

The Schellens collection in the Local History Room of the Redwood City Public Library is astonishing. The bound volumes include: 1. Individuals, 2. Organization and Clubs, 3. Governments and Cities of the county, 4. Communities of San Mateo County and .countiesof The hundreds of 4" boxes contain two or three binders each on shelves that reach 8 feet from the floor and take up two walls of the special reading room. The county binders are alphabetical and go from the most northerly counties to the most southerly counties in the state. A special set of some forty boxes is secure in the vault of the Local History Room. The Archives Board hopes to duplicate and place on the reading room shelves.

The pages in the binders often have but a paragraph from a newspaper page on them and the researcher is expected to then go to the paper and find the complete article.

I wrote this essay in appreciation of Richard N. Schellens and to honor the man who was truly a "History Detective." Those who work with this collection are truly in awe of what this wonderful man accomplished. It is difficult to imagine, when looking at these volumes, how he was able to gather information from all over California for this collection.

The Journal of Local History put out by the archives committee of the Redwood City Public Library.

Volunteers are dedicated to keeping the Local History room open for those who wish to use these valuable assets, the Schellens Collection and the newspapers, the Dennis O'Keefe Collection of original newspapers. The Local History Room also has drawers and drawers of pictures of people, places, houses, fire engines etc. Even so it is hard to find exactly what you are looking for because they didn't take pictures of the farmers; they took pictures of the judges and so forth.

One of the things we are doing to keep Union Cemetery in front of the people in the community is sending out a newsletter at least twice a year. One comes out before Memorial Day in May and the second is an update on what has been accomplished during the year. The members of the cemetery association, pay $10 per year, and receive a copy of the "Journal of Local History" that the archive board sends out three times a year. The Journal of Local History is written and published in the spring, fall and winter of each year. It contains 18 to 24 pages and there is a cemetery story in almost every issue.

Stories in the 2012 Christmas issue include: (1) The True Saint Nicholas, (2) The Ghost at Pigeon Point Lighthouse, (3) Life and Times on the San Francisco Ferry, (4) A Day in the Park Gone Very Wrong, (5) Where's Herbert, (6) Redwood City's Oyster Beds, (7) The Undocumented History of Emerald Lake and (8) The Alaska Codfish Company in Redwood City. Admittedly these stories are of local interest primarily but anybody writing for the purpose of improving an historic cemetery will find; in researching the history of the people buried there, a plethora of really good stories that will literally bring a person back to life. This is especially true if you can find a picture of the individual or a picture of a building or some other recognizable institution or, even a house with which the person was acquainted during his or her life.

One of the most frustrating things in this process is finding photos of women. Few pictures were taken of the average man and, with the exception of well known women; there are no pictures of the fairer sex.

The public is welcome to e-mail gsaurez@redwoodcity.org, he will send you a journal, especially if you commit to a $10 investment which will get you a year's worth of journals.

Enough cannot be said about the Redwood City Department of Parks and Recreation. During this period of economic downturn it has been necessary to lay off a substantial number of employees. None-the-less the department has done a yeoman's job of keeping the cemetery in good shape. They mow the lawns and pick up piles of limbs and other branches and during the spring when the weeds are healthy and we are about to start the cemetery tour events, they spray the weeds well in advance and do everything they can to get the cemetery in good shape.

At the end of April the 150 year old roses are beginning to finish their blooming cycle and the hybrid "T" roses are beginning to bloom. There is about a week when all the 200 plus roses are in bloom. It is a photographer's paradise. It is an absolutely beautiful memorial park, a place to just sit down and relax and look at the beauty that surrounds you.

The plans for this year are several; there is a small curb fence around one of the plots with a curved top. One of the Eagle Scouts has agreed to repair this plot fence. We have earned $3,000 from the "Haunting" last October and this will give us enough to replace two more tombstones, one for Simon Knights, who owned and operated a stage coach line from Redwood City to Pescadero for years, the second for James Van Court who photographed Redwood City and Southern San Mateo County for years. He loved children and photographed them with their musical instruments. He taught them to play those instruments. James Van Court's pictures are, as an immense group, a history of the late 19th century in Redwood City. Vandals have broken off his stone from its base and we will have to study pictures in order to replicate exactly what the original looked like.

In conclusion, this essay is designed to illustrate the procedures that we are using to make improvements in Union Cemetery. This is a city park and it is on the National Register of Historic Places and on the California Historic Landmarks List. Almost any cemetery that contains Civil War dead should be recognized and steps should be taken to improve the occupant's final resting place. I, would be very pleased to hear what processes you have used and what you hope to use in the future. You can reach me through Gene Suarez at, 1044 Middlefield Road, Redwood City, Redwood City, California, 94063.

Final hint: Plant old garden roses, they are far less trouble than hybrid "T" roses, even though they are single bloomers, for the most part. However if you plant roses like Mutablis, which is shown above, which blooms usually 10 months of the year in moderate climates, you have color almost all the time. In Union Cemetery we have both kinds of roses, 44 in all along the fence that parallels Woodside road, State route #84. Drivers see those roses more than any other. There are another 100 or more within the boundaries of the cemetery. When the view is beautiful, many will return with time and look more carefully.

So What's Next for Union Cemetery?

Technology: It is the age of smart phones and pocket computers and the World Wide Internet in every pocket. We will present to the board tomorrow night a proposal to place QR code brackets near the corresponding grave with bar codes. People who come in the cemetery will be able to access the information through the QR readers that most smart phones have when purchased, others will need to add the QR codes to their phones such as I had to do.

The person using the code will be able to read the stories of and families when they have the web site on their phone, www.historicunioncemetery.com for instance if they focus on "Charles

Benjamin and the bar code, they will find out that he was a Civil War soldier who returned to Redwood City after the War and was a member of the San Francisco Board of Supervisors for a period of time. They will also find a picture of Charles in his uniform before he traveled east to fight in the War.

Of course, we do not know if the Cemetery Board will approve the use of this technology. It will be very difficult to conceal the apparatus so the cemetery does not look cluttered. We can only put it together and see if it is worth the effort. Tune into the web-site for ongoing updates on this and other projects.

For example we are trying to replicate and original tomb that has been badly vandalized. These things are always a struggle because the cemetery is on the National Register and we have to be sure we are keeping to the original appearance. The expert fence makers of yore are very hard to duplicate.

People interested in working on similar cemetery sites are invited to contact me through gsuares@redwoodcity.org and he will follow up with me and we will get together over the World Wide Web. I will be happy to help in any way I can.   — John

John G. Edmonds

After high school I joined the U.S. Coast Guard and
served in several duty stations. I completed my four years
of enlistment as Radioman in Charge of the Coast Guard
Cutter Comanche.

I married my present wife, whom I had met in high school,
on March 3, 1962. We were living in an apartment in
Redwood City, CA, when a captain in the Sheriff's offi ce
took up residence as well. After we got to know each other,
he invited me to become a Deputy Sheriff. I did as he
wished and retired from that institution in 2003.

During my entire career of law enforcement, I studied for
scholastic degrees, fi nally completing the studies in 2004
with a doctor's degree in psychology.

www.ingramcontent.com/pod-product-compliance
Lightning Source LLC
Chambersburg PA
CBHW060226290526
45789CB00003B/1426